TRACEY TURNER

STAT ATTACK!

AWESOME ANIMALS

EDGE
FRANKLIN WATTS

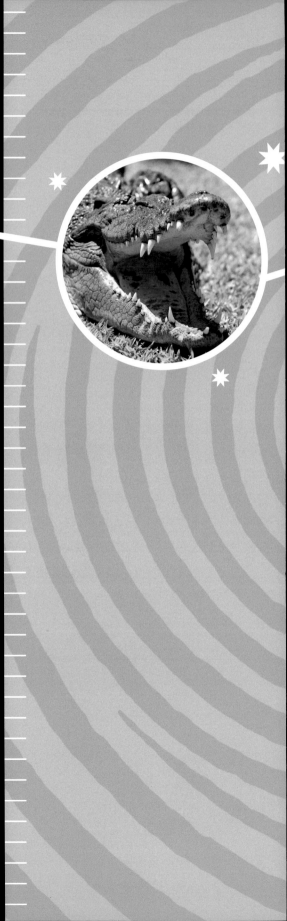

Franklin Watts
Published in Great Britain in 2017 by
The Watts Publishing Group

Credits
Series editor: Adrian Cole
Series designer: Matt Lilly
Art direction: Peter Scoulding
Photo acknowledgements:
aki yoko/Shutterstock: 13br. attem/Shutterstock: 13bl. Fred Bavendam/
Minden Pictures/FLPA: 27tr. Snider Bell/Shutterstock: 12tl. Bhakpong/
Shutterstock: 3tr, 7b. Bios/FLPA: 14bl. Volodymyr Burdiak/Shutterstock: 3tl,
7t, 9c. Sascha Burkard/Shutterstock: front cover c. Patrick K Campbell/
Shutterstock: 19b. Barnaby Chambers/Shutterstock: 12b. Computer Earth/
Shutterstock: 5t. Creativex/Shutterstock: 6cr. Shane Cross/Shutterstock:
5b. Dennis W Donohue/Dreamstime: 16b. Dennis W Donohue/Shutterstock:
9b, 23. E B Photo/Shutterstock: 10bl. Ecoprint/Shutterstock: 8tl. Tim
Edwards/Nature P L: 20. e2dan/Shutterstock: 11b. Nick Everett/Dreamstime:
26b. Flash-ka/Shutterstock: 14t. Jurgen Freund/Nature P L: 24b. Daniel
Heuclin/Nature P L: 19c. Eric Isselee/Shutterstock: 15t, 18tl. Anton Ivanov/
Shutterstock: 18b. Jeep5d/Dreamstime: 2, 8tr, 10tr. Judex/Shutterstock:
front cover cl, 15c. Johann Larson/Shutterstock: 15b. Kanokratnok/
Shutterstock: 21t. Robert L Kothenbeutel/Shutterstock: 22t. Bernd Leitner
Fotodesign/Shutterstock: 24t. Tiaw Leong Lim/Dreamstime: 27tl. Timothy
Lubecke/Dreamstime: 16tl. Matt9122/Shutterstock: 26t. Stephan Morris/
Shutterstock: 14cl. outdoors man/Shutterstock: 8b. Boris Pamikov/
Shutterstock: 21br. Komkrich Patchusiri/Shutterstock: front cover cr. Sean
Pavone/Shutterstock: 19t. photobar/Shutterstock: 22b. Photo Research/
FLPA: 18tr. Yusran Abdul Rahman/Shutterstock: 11t. Donovan van Stedjen/
Shutterstock: 1, 6cl. Steve Trewhella/FLPA: 14cr. Wacpan/Shutterstock: 13t.
worldwildlifewonders/Shutterstock: 16tr. Erik Zandboer/Shutterstock: 21cl.
Hongqi Zhang/Dreamstime: 25t.

Every attempt has been made to clear copyright. Should there be any inad-
vertent omission please apply to the publisher for rectification.

Dewey number 590
ISBN 978 1 4451 2754 5

Printed in China

MIX
Paper from
responsible sources
FSC® C104740
FSC
www.fsc.org

Franklin Watts
An imprint of
Hachette Children's Group
Part of The Watts Publishing Group
Carmelite House
50 Victoria Embankment
London EC4Y 0DZ

An Hachette UK Company
www.hachette.co.uk

www.franklinwatts.co.uk

CONTENTS

Introduction

Did you just hear a sort of straining kind of noise? It's probably because this book is bursting with information about the world's most awesome animals. In it you'll discover information about animals that are huge, tiny, deadly, toxic, smelly and slimy. Quake with terror as you meet a fearsome predator with three hundred teeth, and shudder with disgust at the animal that creates a shower of its own poo. Find out about monster rodents, deadly snakes, venomous caterpillars and toxic frogs.

As well as facts and stats, there are quizzes to test your animal knowledge. In fact, let's have one now. Before you start reading the book, see if you can answer these questions:

1) Which animal has the strongest bite of any mammal?

2) Which is the sea creature that kills the most people each year?

3) Which animal is the world's best long-distance runner?

Read on to find out if you're right.

Prepare to stuff your brain with hundreds of amazing facts and statistics until it's ready to explode! (Actually, we should point out here that the publishers take no responsibility whatsoever for exploding brains.)

15 Enormous Animals

These whoppers of the animal kingdom are listed in order of weight.

1 Blue Whale

The blue whale is the biggest animal there's ever been – much bigger than any dinosaur. Just its tongue weighs as much as an especially hefty rhinoceros, and its heart is as big as a car. To fuel its giant body, it eats tiny shrimp-like creatures called krill. It sieves them out of seawater using special filters in its jaw, called baleen.

STAT ATTACK!

Maximum length: 32 m	
Maximum weight: 180 tonnes	
Weight of tongue: 4 tonnes	
Size of newborn baby blue whale: up to 8 m long and 2.7 tonnes in weight	
Where it's found: worldwide	

MORE WHOPPING GREAT WHALES

2 Fin Whale

STAT ATTACK!

Maximum length: 26 m	
Maximum weight: 80 tonnes	

3 Right Whale

STAT ATTACK!

Maximum length: 15 m	
Maximum weight: 65 tonnes	

Like blue whales, both fin and right whales are baleen whales.

4 Sperm Whale

STAT ATTACK!

Maximum length: 20 m	
Maximum weight: 50 tonnes	
Average size of brain: 8,000 cubic cm	
Where it's found: worldwide	

There are bigger whales (see above), but sperm whales can boast that they have the world's biggest heads, and the biggest brains ever to have existed. They're also the largest animals in the world that have teeth. They can dive nearly 2 km deep, and prey on animals including giant squid.

5 Whale shark

The biggest shark on Earth is 5 m longer than a great white. But relax, it doesn't even have teeth. It filters its food, mostly plankton and very small fish, through its enormous gaping mouth. Even if you swam into it by mistake, its throat isn't big enough to swallow you.

STAT ATTACK!

Maximum length: 12 m	
Maximum weight: 20 tonnes	
Maximum width of mouth: 1.5 m	
Where it's found: tropical seas	

6 Elephant

The African elephant is the world's biggest land animal, and is so strong it can push over trees and pick up tree trunks. Even a newborn baby elephant can weigh 120 kg. Never mess with an African elephant: they can charge at 40 kph when they're cross!

STAT ATTACK!

Maximum height: 4.2 m	
Maximum length: 7 m	
Maximum weight: 12.25 tonnes	
Maximum length of tusk: 3.5 m	
Where it's found: Africa	

7 Elephant seal

Southern elephant seals are a bit like elephants because they're absolutely massive and their noses look like very short, stubby trunks. Male elephant seals are much bigger than the females, who have to stay out of the way when the males have one of their regular nasty fights, sometimes to the death.

STAT ATTACK!

Maximum length: 6 m	
Maximum weight: 4 tonnes	
Where it's found: southern elephant seals are found in Antarctica; northern elephant seals are found in western North America	

8 Rhinocerous

Africa has more than its fair share of huge land animals: the white rhino is one of them. It's the second largest after the elephant. Not only is it ginormous, but it also has an extremely impressive horn on the end of its nose – rhinos are the only land animals to have one. That's just showing off!

STAT ATTACK!

Maximum height: 2 m

Maximum length: 4.5 m

Maximum weight: 4 tonnes.

Maximum speed: 50 kph

Maximum length of horn: 1.5 m

Where it's found: Africa

9 Hippopotamus

Hippos are the third largest land animals, and one of the most feared animals in Africa. Although they are vegetarian, they're aggressive and are easily upset. They have the strongest bite of any mammal and can (and regularly do) kill people. They also have some nasty habits, including twirling their tails to create a shower of poo to mark their territory.

STAT ATTACK!

Maximum height: 1.75 m

Maximum length: 5 m

Maximum weight: 3 tonnes

Maximum length of longest tooth: 60 cm

Maximum width of open mouth: 1 m

Where it's found: sub-Saharan Africa

10 Giraffe

The world's tallest land animal has a ridiculously long neck, which is almost certainly longer than the tallest person you know. Giraffes also have long, rubbery, blue tongues for grabbing leaves to eat.

STAT ATTACK!

Maximum height: 6 m	
Maximum length: 4.5 m	
Maximum weight: 1.9 tonnes	
Maximum neck length: 2.5 m	
Maximum length of tongue: 50 cm	
Where it's found: Africa	

11 Saltwater crocodile

This terrifying beast is the world's largest reptile. Saltwater crocodiles have the second strongest bite of any animal (after the great white shark) and regularly eat people.

STAT ATTACK!

Maximum length: 7 m	
Maximum weight: 1 tonne	
Length of teeth: 9 cm	

Where it's found: northern Australia, eastern India and Bangladesh, Indonesia and Malaysia, New Guinea, Myanmar and some South Pacific islands.

12 Polar bear

The polar bear is the world's largest predator, hunting seals, fish, caribou and anything else it can lay its giant paws on in the Arctic. It  has keen senses, especially its sense of smell, and can sniff out seals in dens under the snow.

STAT ATTACK!

Maximum length: 2.5 m (standing up to 3 m on hind legs)	
Maximum weight: 1 tonne	
Maximum speed: 40 kph	
Where it's found: Arctic	

13 Colossal squid

This enormous creature has never been seen alive: it lives in the depths of the ocean, where it eats fish and other squid. We only know about it because dead colossal squid have been washed up on the shore. Its eyes are the biggest in the animal kingdom – each is the size of a football. It has eight arms, plus two tentacles that grab prey on sharp hooks and feed it into its beak-like mouth.

STAT ATTACK!

Maximum length: 14 m

Maximum weight: 495 kg

Length of arms: 1 m

Diameter of eyeball: 27 cm

Where it's found: deep waters of the Southern Ocean

14 Tiger

The Siberian tiger is the biggest cat in the world. As tigers have been known to eat people, there are a few things you should know: despite their massive size, tigers can run very fast – chasing deer, wild pigs and smaller prey – and can leap up to 5 m high. Unlike most other cats, tigers like water and are good swimmers.

STAT ATTACK!

Maximum length: 2.1 m long, plus tail up to 1 metre long

Maximum weight: 300 kg

Maximum speed: 60 kph

Where it's found: eastern Russia and northern China

15 Gorilla

Gorillas are the world's biggest primates. They aren't especially tall, but they make up for it in massive muscly power, and weigh as much as four men. These gentle giants live in the rainforest in big family groups, spending up to 14 hours a day eating plants (though big males fight each other using their long, sharp fangs).

STAT ATTACK!

Maximum height: 1.8 m

Maximum weight: 275 kg

Waist measurement: 1.7 m

Where it's found: Central and East Africa

AWESOME ANIMALS QUIZ

Use the Internet to help research the answers to these questions.

1 Which is the world's biggest fish?

a) Whale shark

b) Blue whale

c) Fin whale

d) Colossal squid

2 A crocodile is a what?

a) Mammal

b) Reptile

c) Amphibian

d) None of the above

3 Which animal has the biggest brain in the world – EVER?

a) Elephant   b) Giraffe   c) Sperm whale   d) Rhinocerous

4 Which of these animals has the most powerful bite?

a) Hippopotamus   b) Polar bear

c) Saltwater crocodile   d) Tiger

5 What does a gorilla spend most of its day doing?

a) Sleeping   b) Eating

c) Running

d) Building up its muscles

6 Which of these can grow a complete new body from just one arm and a small piece of the centre of its body?

a) Octopus   b) Starfish   c) Squid   d) Cuttlefish

7 What's unusual about the blue-ringed octopus **(apart from its blue rings)?**

a) It has ten arms instead of eight

b) It lights up at night   c) Its bite is deadly

d) It only eats venomous sea snakes

8 What does **the** vampire squid **feed on?**

a) Other types of squid

b) Poo and dead bodies

c) Prawns and small fish

d) Blood

9 Giant isopods, **40 cm long and found in the deep sea,** are most similar to which of these land creatures?

a) Praying mantis

b) Woodlouse

c) Spider

d) Grasshopper

10 Sea pigs **are?**

a) Sea cucumbers with legs

b) Round-bodied sharks

c) Fish with snout-like noses   d) Fish with curly tails

Awesome answers **on page 30**

11

Two absolutely
ENORMOUS SPIDERS

Have you ever seen a big spider scuttling across the carpet and shrieked? The chances are it was just a tiny baby compared to these huge, hairy monsters.

1
The Goliath Bird-eating Spider

This bird-eating spider is massive, by anybody's standards. It's also known as a tarantula, and has monster fangs that can deliver a nasty bite. Its venom isn't strong enough for it to kill a person, but if you're a mouse you'd better watch out.

STAT ATTACK!

* Maximum legspan: 30 cm
* Maximum weight: 175 g
* Length of body: 12 cm
* Length of fangs: 2.5 cm
* Where it's found: South America

2
The Giant Huntsman Spider

This spider was only discovered in 2001 – it had been hiding in dark caves in Laos up until then. It has the same maximum legspan as the Goliath bird-eating spider, but it's nowhere near as chunky – its body is smaller, and its long legs are much thinner. You'll be relieved to know it's not dangerous to people.

STAT ATTACK!

* Maximum legspan: 30 cm
* Body length: 4.5 cm
* Where it's found: Laos, south-east Asia

12

THREE MORE SHUDDER-INDUCING
CREEPY CRAWLIES

If creepy-crawlies freak you out, you might want to look away at this point.

1. CAMEL SPIDER

Camel spiders aren't really spiders at all – they're solpugids, which are arachnids, like scorpions and spiders, but not the same. They're hairy, extremely ugly, and have the largest jaws in relation to their size of any animal in the world. They can deliver a nasty bite, too (although it won't kill you, apparently).

STAT ATTACK!
Size: Up to 15 cm

STAT ATTACK!
Where it's found: N. Africa and the Middle East

2. GIANT CENTIPEDE

STAT ATTACK!
Number of legs: 46   Size: 30 cm

Centipedes are bad enough when they're a few centimetres long, but aggressive giant ones that deliver a venomous bite are just plain wrong. They also have far too many legs.

STAT ATTACK!
Where it's found: S. America

3. JAPANESE GIANT HORNET

The sting of these huge hornets is incredibly painful and can even be fatal if several of them sting.

STAT ATTACK!
Size: 5 cm

Wingspan: 7.5 cm

Where found: Japan

SLIMY & SMELLY QUIZ!

Use the Internet to help research the answers to these questions.

1
The Tasmanian devil **stinks of . . .**

a) Rotting meat   **b)** Bad eggs   **c)** Cabbage

2 **Which of these is a defence tactic of the** striped polecat**?**

a) Spitting foul-smelling toxic liquid

b) Playing dead with foul-smelling liquid coming from its mouth, nose and bottom

c) Dancing on hind legs while pooing uncontrollably

3 **Where does a** violet sea snail **live?**

a) Suspended upside-down from a raft of slime bubbles

b) Next to a shark's bottom

c) In a rock pool filled with its own slime

4
How far can a skunk **fire its foul-smelling liquid?**

a) 50 cm   **b)** 1 m   **c)** 6 m

5
The slimiest creature in the world, the hagfish**, is also known as the . . .**

a) Slithering ghoul   **b)** Snot eel   **c)** Slime muncher

    Vile answers **on page 30**

1 GOLDEN POISON FROG

The tiny golden poison frog, possibly the most poisonous creature in the world, is very rare. If you touch one (let alone eat it) the poison could easily reach your bloodstream and kill you. Some South American tribespeople use poison from poison frogs' skin to coat their arrow tips.

STAT ATTACK!

Size: 4.5 cm

Enough poison to kill: 10 adult humans

Where it's found: Colombian rainforest

2 PUFFER FISH

When a puffer fish is threatened, it fills its stomach with water to 'puff' up its spikey body. Predators are put off by the spikes, and also the larger, puffed-up fish. There are chefs in Japan who have trained for years to cut away the poisonous bits of puffer fish so people in posh restaurants can eat them.

STAT ATTACK!

Size: 2.5 cm to 60 cm

Enough poison to kill: 30 adult humans (the most toxic kind is much bigger than a golden poison frog)

Where it's found: warmer waters worldwide

MORE POISONOUS CREATURES:

3 CANE TOADS

Some of the biggest toads on Earth release foul-tasting poison when threatened. They're from South America but have been introduced to lots of other countries.

4 PITOHUI AND IFRITA BIRDS

There aren't many poisonous birds, but two of them are from Papua New Guinea. Their skin and feathers contain toxins.

5 INLAND TAIPAN SNAKE

The inland taipan is one of the most venomous snakes in the world. Luckily it's shy and doesn't often come into contact with people.

STAT ATTACK!

Size: up to 1.8 m	
Enough venom to kill: 100 adult humans	
Where it's found: central Australia	

6 DUCK-BILLED PLAYTPUS

What? Really? Oh yes. The duck-billed platypus is weird in many different ways, and it also happens to be the world's most venomous mammal (as well as one of only two egg-laying ones, and the only one with a bill like a duck's). It has a barb on its hind leg that injects poison, and although it's very painful it's not powerful enough to kill a person.

STAT ATTACK!

Size: up to 50 cm (including tail)	
Enough venom to kill: 0 adult humans	
Where it's found: eastern Australia	

MORE VENOMOUS CREATURES:

7 DEATHSTALKER SCORPIONS

Deathstalker scorpions are the most venomous scorpions – but they're not likely to kill a grown human being unless the person is ill.

8 CATERPILLARS

Some caterpillars are venomous, injecting poison through their hairs, and one has been known to kill people – a mega-hairy giant silkworm moth, *Lonomia obliqua*, found in South America.

Have a look on pages 13 and 24 for more venomous creatures.

1. Insect

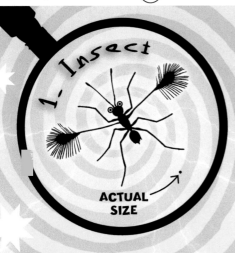

ACTUAL SIZE

The fairy wasp is so unbelievably titchy that there are bigger single-celled organisms, yet the wasp has wings and legs and everything. They lay their eggs on the eggs of other small insects, then the fairy wasp larvae eat the host egg when they hatch.

STAT ATTACK!
Fairy wasp size:
0.4 mm

2. Frog

ACTUAL SIZE

Discovered in 2009 in remote rainforest, the Amau frog is so tiny it could fit on the tip of your thumb. As well as the world's smallest frog, it's also the smallest vertebrate (backboned animal). It lives on the damp forest floor, where it eats insects – really small ones, obviously.

STAT ATTACK!
Amau frog size:
8 mm

3. Bird

ACTUAL SIZE

The bee hummingbird could be a pimple on the bottom of an ostrich, the world's largest bird (well, almost). It isn't really as small as a bee (the largest bee in the world is about a centimetre smaller), but it's only half the size of the world's biggest insect (see page 20).

STAT ATTACK!
Bee hummingbird size:
5 cm, 2 grams

4. Monkey

The pygmy marmoset lives in the rainforests of Central and South America, and is smaller than the biggest beetle that lives there (see page 20).

STAT ATTACK!

Pygmy marmoset average size: 15 cm (plus a 20-cm-long tail), 100 g

5. Bat

ACTUAL SIZE

The bumblebee bat, or Kitti's hog-nosed bat, is also the world's smallest mammal, and makes the mouse lemur look like a giant. It lives in Thailand and Myanmar.

STAT ATTACK!

Bumblebee bat size: 4 cm, 2 g

Monkey Puzzle

How much do you know about your hairier relatives?

True or False?

1. The howler monkey's call can be heard 5 km away.
2. The proboscis monkey has unusually large ears.
3. Each of a tarsier's eyes is bigger than its brain.
4. Chimps have the most complex animal calls.
5. Packs of gorillas use teamwork to hunt monkeys.
6. Capuchin monkeys use tools to crack nuts.
7. Monkeys were responsible for the death of a politician in 2007.
8. Gorillas are completely vegetarian.

Hairy answers on page 31

10 Animals
That Are Far Too Big

It's fine for things like whales and elephants to be huge – that's completely fair enough.

But crabs the size of ponies? Snakes as long as buses? Stop it!

1 Japanese spider crab

These massive crabs have a leg span as long as a small car!

STAT ATTACK!

Maximum legspan: 3.8 m

Maximum weight: 19 kg

Where it's found: coastal Japan

2 Chinese giant salamander

Salamanders are amphibians, like frogs, and look like lizards. Most of them are smaller than your hand, but this one is the size of an adult human being.

STAT ATTACK!

Maximum length: 1.8 m

Maximum weight: 50 kg

Where it's found: China

3 Green anaconda

This huge snake is the biggest in the world. (Reticulated pythons can be even longer than anacondas, but aren't as heavy.) It's a constricting snake, which means it coils its immense body around its prey and squeezes it to death, then eats it whole.

STAT ATTACK!

Maximum length: 9 m

Maximum weight: 230 kg

Maximum waist measurement: 1 m

Where it's found: South America

4 Little Barrier Giant Weta

Giant wetas are the world's heaviest insects. They look like huge grasshoppers, though they're too heavy to jump or fly as they weigh the same as an average gerbil. They can bite through a carrot, but don't usually bite people.

✳ STAT ATTACK!

Maximum length: 10 cm	Maximum legspan: 20 cm
Maximum weight: 70 g ✳	Where it's found: Little Barrier Island, New Zealand

Three more incredibly large insects

5 Goliath beetle

The world's heaviest flying insect is the Goliath beetle, which lives in Central Africa – it's 12 cm long with a wingspan of 25 cm, and weighs 60 g. ✳

6 Titan beetle

The Titan beetle of South America can reach 16.7 cm long.

7 Hercules beetle

The Hercules beetle can be up to 17.5 cm, though it's cheating quite a bit because that also includes its massive horn.

✳

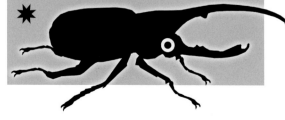

8 Capybara

No rodent should be this large! The capybara looks like a monster guinea pig and is the world's biggest rodent. It eats grass and other vegetation and, like rabbits, it also eats its own poo to get maximum nutrition from its food. (Sorry if you're reading this just after eating your lunch.) *

STAT ATTACK!

Maximum length: 1.2 m *

Maximum height: 65 cm

Maximum weight: 65 kg

Where it's found: Central and South America

9 * Giant fruit bat *

Bats are small flying mammals that flit about at night eating insects, right? Well, not these beauties. The biggest types of fruit bat (also known as flying foxes or megabats) have enormous wings and live on fruit and nectar. The one with the biggest wingspan is the large flying fox.

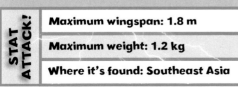

STAT ATTACK!

Maximum wingspan: 1.8 m

Maximum weight: 1.2 kg

Where it's found: Southeast Asia

10 * Lion's mane * jellyfish

It's bad enough that they can sting, so jellyfish should, by rights, stick to being a manageable size. This one definitely isn't. Luckily, its sting is fatal to fish, but not to us.

STAT ATTACK!

Maximum size: 2.2 m across

Maximum length: 30 m

Where it's found: northern seas and seas around Australia and New Zealand

The World's Three Fastest Animals

1st Peregrine falcon

The fastest animal in the world zooms through the air in a death-defying hunting dive called a stoop. Peregrines whack into their prey at such a speed that they stun or even kill it on impact. Then they grab it and fly off (more slowly) to devour it.

STAT ATTACK!

Maximum speed:	320 kph
Length:	50 cm
Wingspan:	1.2 m
Where it's found:	worldwide

2nd Cheetah

The cheetah is the world's fastest land animal. The speedy big cat whizzes along faster than the motorway speed limit and accelerates faster than an ordinary car. As it sprints, the cheetah covers more than 7 m in a single bound. It sprints for short distances to catch its prey, which is mainly small hoofed animals like gazelles, but can't keep up the amazing pace for very long.

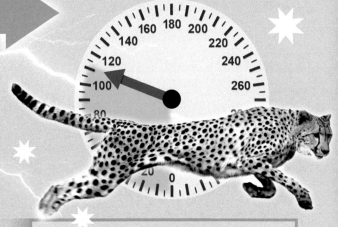

STAT ATTACK!

Maximum speed:	114 kph
Length:	2 m, plus tail up to 85 cm long
Weight:	60 kg
Where it's found:	southern and eastern Africa

3rd ‾Pronghorn

The pronghorn, a deer-like animal, is the second-fastest land animal, racing along at a top speed of 86 kph. It can keep up a speed of 65 kph for twenty minutes, so it's the best long-distance runner on the planet. If it kept going at that speed it would finish a marathon in less than forty minutes.

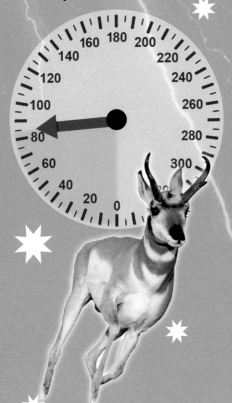

STAT ATTACK!

Maximum speed: 86 kph	
Length: 1.5 m	
Height: 1 m	
Weight: 68 kg	
Where it's found: North America	

‾Super Speedy ‾Quiz

USE THE INTERNET TO HELP RESEARCH THE ANSWERS TO THESE QUESTIONS.

1 A cheetah's **resting heart rate is 16 beats per minute. What is it when a cheetah is sprinting?**

a) 36   **b)** 96   **c)** 150

2 **Which of these animals prey on** pronghorn**?**

a) Mountain lions

b) Cheetahs

c) Leopards

3 **How does a** peregrine falcon **usually stun its prey?**

a) With its head

b) With its beak

c) With its foot

Speedy answers **on page 31**

23

Plenty of sea creatures are deadly to other sea creatures,
but what about the ones we need to worry about?

If you're planning a trip to the beach, make sure one of these isn't lying in
wait beneath the surface of the waves, or lurking in a rock pool.

1 SALTWATER CROCODILE

These monster crocs – the biggest
reptiles in the world – lurk in fresh water
and sea water, just to keep you guessing.
The bigger ones wouldn't think twice
about grabbing and eating a human
being, and frequently do.

On average, more than 60 people are killed every year
by saltwater crocodiles. See the Stat Attack on page 8.

2 BOX JELLYFISH

Box jellyfish are difficult to see
because they're transparent, but
their trailing tentacles can kill you.
This is not a good combination, and
there's more bad news: box jellies'
venom is one of the most toxic on the
planet, and the agonising pain of the
sting can stop a person's heart. Box
jellyfish, also known as sea wasps,
are a bit more sophisticated than
true jellyfish – they have eyes and
can move themselves about to catch
their fishy prey, rather than just
drifting.

STAT ATTACK!

Maximum body size: 25 cm

Maximum length including tentacles: 3 m

Maximum weight: 2 kg

Where they're found: mainly in northern
Australia and the Indo-Pacific

Numbers are difficult to come by, but there have been more
than 70 confirmed human deaths in the sea around Australia,
and there are probably more than ten a year worldwide.

③ SHARKS

TIGER SHARK

You might have thought sharks would be higher up the list, but in fact they only munch an average of around six people a year. The three sharks most likely to finish you off – and it might be hard to tell through all that red foam and thrashing – are great whites, tiger sharks and bull sharks. Of course, there are other sharks that might want to take a bite given the chance. Tiger sharks are famous for eating anything. Bull sharks aren't fussy either, plus they're aggressive and tend to live near the coast.

Great whites are the biggest sharks and have the strongest bite of any creature, but apparently they're picky eaters, and might not fancy the rest of you once they've taken a bite – though that's not necessarily good news, for obvious reasons.

STAT ATTACK!

Tiger shark:
Maximum length: 7 m
Maximum weight: 900 kg
Where they're found: worldwide

Great white shark:
Maximum length: 6 m
Maximum weight: 2.2 tonnes
Maximum speed: 40 kph
Where they're found: worldwide

Bull shark:
Maximum length: 3.5 m
Maximum weight: 230 kg
Where they're found: worldwide

 On average only about 6 people are killed by sharks each year.

▷ STINGRAY

4

Stingrays are sharks' relatives, and there are lots of different types. Most have a sharp venomous barb in their tail, which they use to defend themselves.

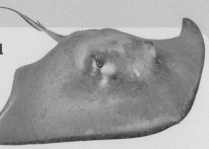

✸ STAT ATTACK!

Maximum length: 2.5 m

Maximum weight: 350 kg

Where it's found: seas (and some rivers) worldwide, apart from polar seas

☠ Don't worry: stingrays aren't usually dangerous, and there are very few reported human deaths.

▷ BLUE-RINGED OCTOPUS

5

Blue-ringed octopus are only the size of a tennis ball, yet they can kill you with one bite due to their highly toxic venom. You'd have to really annoy one first, though (you'll know if you have, because its blue rings start to glow).

✸ STAT ATTACK!

Maximum length: 20 cm (largest species)

Where it's found: Pacific and Indian oceans, Japan to Australia

 ☠ There are only a handful of recorded human deaths from the octopus's bite.

6 ▷ STONEFISH

Stonefish are the world's most venomous fish. They're so well camouflaged that you might not spot them among rocks and stones near the sea shore. They can raise venomous spines on their backs. The venom is so powerful that it can kill a person if not treated in time.

STAT ATTACK!

Maximum length:
50 cm

Number of venomous spines:
13

Where it's found:
tropical seas

 Most people survive, only suffering agonising pain for a few hours.

7 ▷ CONE SNAIL

Cone snails live in just the sort of pretty shell you might want to pick up, but don't be tempted. The most toxic kind, the geographic cone snail, can inject deadly venom that kills in minutes through a harpoon-like tube.

STAT ATTACK!

Maximum size:
20 cm

Where it's found:
parts of Pacific and Indian oceans

 There are very few recorded deaths by cone snail.

Deadly Animal Qui

Use the Internet to help research the answers to these questions.

1 Which of these carnivores **have been spotted swimming hundreds of kilometres from land?**

a) Tigers **b)** Polar bears

c) Weasels **d)** Tasmanian devils

2 Which of these sharks **has over 300 rows of teeth?**

a) Great white shark

b) Whale shark

c) Basking shark

d) Sand tiger shark

3 Which of these big cats **have the loudest roar?**

a) Tiger **b)** Leopard

c) Lion **d)** Cheetah

4 Which of these lizards **has been known to attack and kill people?**

a) Gila monster **b)** Gecko

c) Komodo dragon **d)** Skink

5 Which of these hunt **as a team?**

a) Tigers **b)** Lions **c)** Jaguars **d)** Pumas

6 Which of these is responsible for more human deaths **per year than any other?**

a) Crocodiles | **b)** Hippos | **c)** Snakes | **d)** Sharks

7 Which type of shark has been found with car number plates, fur coats, shoes and other rubbish inside its stomach?

a) Ocean white tip shark

b) Nurse shark

c) Lemon shark

d) Tiger shark

FEB BFWS215

8 Which of these spiders **is the most dangerous to people?**

a) Black widow

b) Goliath tarantula

c) Brazilian wandering spider

d) Wolf spider

9 Which of these creepy-crawlies **is the deadliest?**

a) Giant centipede

b) Death stalker scorpion

c) Red-back spider

d) Mosquito

10 Which is the largest venomous snake **in the world?**

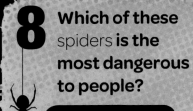

a) King cobra

b) Inland taipan

c) Reticulated python

d) Carpet viper

Deadly answers **on page 31**

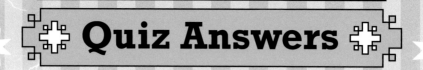

Quiz Answers

AWESOME ANIMALS ANSWERS (PAGES 10–11)

1a) At up to 12 m long, the whale shark is the biggest fish, but the oarfish is the world's longest bony fish, at around 11 m. The blue whale, fin whale and colossal squid aren't fish.

2b) A crocodile is a reptile. They are believed to have survived since the time of the dinosaurs, some 20 million years ago.

3c) The animal with the largest brain – ever – is the sperm whale. It can hold its breath for 90 minutes and dive down 1,000 m to feed on its favourite food: squid.

4c) Saltwater crocodile's have the most powerful bite at 3,700 psi (pounds per square inch). You, on the other hand, have a bite pressure of just 150–200 psi.

5b) Gorillas spend most of their time eating. They are herbivores, and eat leaves, shoots, roots, vines and fruits.

6b) Some types of starfish can grow a completely new body like this, and most can regenerate a new arm if they lose one.

7c) Its bite is deadly. If you see a blue-ringed octopus's blue rings beginning to glow, watch out, because it means it's getting ready to bite. The venom can kill a person in minutes!

8b) A more polite way of saying it would be 'organic matter floating in the sea'. The vampire squid looks more menacing than it actually is.

9b) It's just like a giant underwater woodlouse.

10a) Sea pigs are a type of sea cucumber, and are related to starfish and sea urchins.

SLIMY & SMELLY ANSWERS (PAGE 14)

1a) Tasmanian devils often eat dead animals, so they probably like it.

2b) It plays dead to confuse predators. The liquid can temporarily blind them, or make them run away.

3a)

4b) It can spray 1 m, but the foul-smelling mist will travel 3 m. It squirts it from a gland under its tail.

5b)

Monkey Puzzle Answers (page 18)

1) True – they're the loudest animal on land (whales make more noise underwater).

2) False – they have huge, floppy noses.

3) True – tarsiers are nocturnal and need their enormous eyes to help them see in the dark.

4) False – gelada baboons have the most complex communication sounds we know of.

5) False – packs of chimps do, though.

6) True – capuchins use stones and logs to crack nuts. Various types of monkey and ape can use tools.

7) True! Rhesus monkeys attacked the Deputy Mayor of Delhi and he fell off a balcony.

8) False – gorillas also eat ants, termites, worms and grubs.

Super Speedy Answers (page 23)

1c) A cheetah's body is under so much strain when it's sprinting that it has to have a rest before it can eat the animal it's just caught!

2a) Pronghorns live in North America, so there aren't any cheetahs and leopards to chase them.

3c) Peregrines usually whack their prey with a closed foot, before grabbing it in sharp, curved talons.

Deadly Animal Answers (PAGES 28–29)

1) Polar bears have been seen hundreds of kilometres out to sea – they probably caught a lift on floating ice sheets for some of the way.

2a) Whale sharks have about 4,000 tiny teeth, but none of them are sharp. The whale shark is a filter feeder, and feeds mostly on plankton.

3c) A lion's roar can be heard over 8 km away.

4c) Komodo dragons have been known to kill people. They are the world's largest lizard, and have a venomous bite full of lethal bacteria.

5b) Lions are the only big cats to hunt in groups.

6c) There are more than 10,000 human deaths from snake bites every year in India alone. The two worst offenders are the Indian cobra and Russell's viper. In Africa, puff adders, carpet vipers and Egyptian cobras cause hundreds of human deaths per year.

7d) Tiger sharks are sometimes known as the dustbins of the sea. One was found with part of a suit of armour in its stomach.

8c) Brazilian wandering spiders are aggressive, they can jump, and they have an extremely venomous bite that can kill if it's not treated quickly.

9d) The bite of an Anopheles mosquito spreads the disease malaria, caused by a parasite, which kills millions of people. There were 600,000 deaths from malaria in 2012 alone.

10a) King cobras can grow up to 5.7 m long. Reticulated pythons are the longest snakes (up to 10.2 m), but they're not venomous.

GLOSSARY

arachnid – A member of the group of animals without backbones (invertebrates).

barb – In animals, a pointed or hooked part of the body.

carnivore – An animal that feeds on other animals.

krill – A small, shrimp-like animal (crustacean) that lives in the sea.

larva – The name for a stage in the life cycle of many insects – egg, larva, adult.

nectar – The liquid produced in plant flowers to encourage insects or animals to visit the flower and pollinate it.

plankton – Tiny living things that drift and float in the sea or in fresh water.

predator – An animal that preys on others in order to hunt and kill them for food.

primate – A member of the group of mammals that includes apes and lemurs.

reticulated – A criss-cross pattern.

rodent – A member of the group of gnawing mammals that includes rats and squirrels.

sea cucumber – An animal with a long body, many legs and tentacles around its mouth that lives on the sea floor.

single-celled organism – The most simple form of living thing.

territory – The area of land defended by an animal, or a group of animals.

venomous – Able to inject poison (venom).

INDEX